THE BEST OF
GOLDEN OAK FURNITURE
WITH DETAILS AND PRICES

Schiffer Publishing Ltd

4880 Lower Valley Road, Atglen, PA 19310 USA

The Best of
GOLDEN OAK FURNITURE
WITH DETAILS AND PRICES

Nancy N. Schiffer

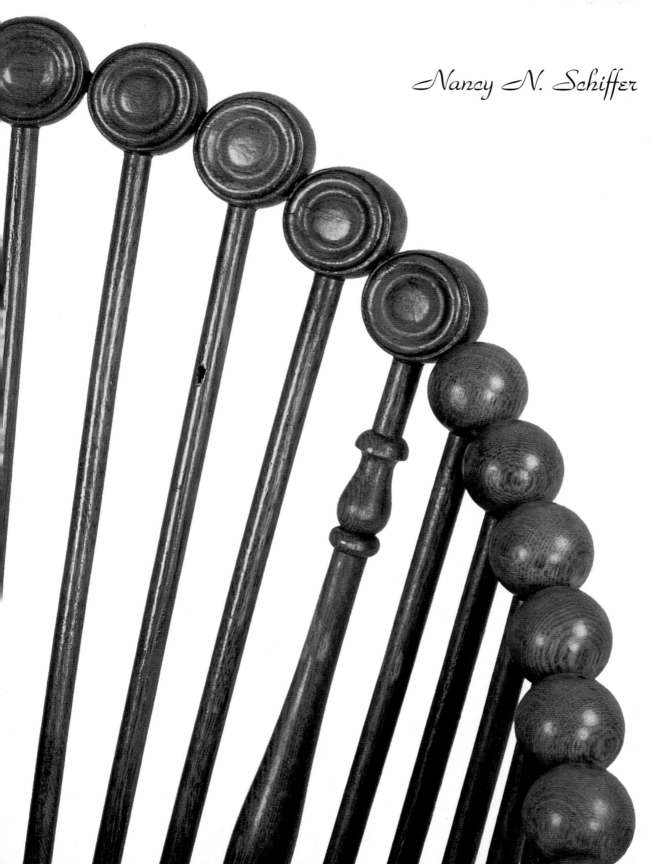

Copyright © 2000 by Nancy N. Schiffer
Library of Congress Catalog Card Number: 00-101392

Book Design by Blair R. Loughrey
Type set in Park Avenue/Americana/Zurich

ISBN: 0-7643-1147-6
Printed in China

Published by Schiffer Publishing Ltd.
4880 Lower Valley Road
Atglen, PA 19310
Phone: (610) 593-1777; Fax: (610) 593-2002
E-mail: Schifferbk@aol.com
Please visit our web site catalog at
WWW.SCHIFFERBOOKS.COM
We are always looking for people to write books on new and related subjects. If you have an idea for a book, please contact us at the above address.

This book may be purchased from the publisher.
Include $3.95 for shipping. Please try your bookstore first.
You may write for a free catalog.

In Europe, Schiffer books are distributed by
Bushwood Books
6 Marksbury Ave. Kew Gardens
Surrey TW9 4JF England
Phone: 44 (0)208-392-8585; Fax: 44 (0)208-392-9876
E-mail: Bushwd@aol.com
Free postage in the UK. Europe: air mail at cost.
Please try your bookstore first.

Contents

ACKNOWLEDGMENTS

Woodcarvers and furniture collectors alike requested a book about high quality oak furniture and its carved details. Both groups felt it would be very useful in their studies of wood, both as decorative and useful objects.

Dean Grimshaw of the Hobbit Shop Antiques, in Naches, Washington, tel. 509-965-0768, has been a dealer in fine oak furniture for many years. He has specialized in handling the finest forms of the late nineteenth century, and oak furniture in particular. He enthusiastically matched his collection and archives with our interest, and made the opportunity to photograph his collection a reality. We are sincerely grateful to Dean, his wife Susie, and son Mark for all their cooperation, shared knowledge, and encouragement during the preparation of this book.

INTRODUCTION

The idea to present a book about high quality oak furniture and its carving details emerged from conversations with present-day woodworkers who wanted to study the past in order to interpret the present in their work. Collectors of furniture added that they wanted to see these details clearly, too, because differences in carving skills can relate directly to the compositions and values of otherwise comparable pieces.

The oak furniture presented here is outstanding in its superior proportions, quality workmanship, and carving details. It is the result of two dynamic forces developing at the end of the nineteenth century in America. First, the furniture industry, from the 1870s forward, became ever more mechanized and skilled to produce high quality forms at competitive prices. Second, the growing clientele of increasingly wealthy people demanded superior, ever-more elaborate furniture. As incomes increased, houses grew

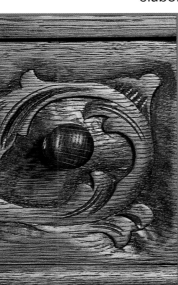

larger and social pressures enticed people to show their wealth with more elaborate and more numerous personal possessions. They accumulated more books, dishes, and clothing for which they wanted more bookcases, china cabinets, and chests of drawers. They displayed more silver and cut glass serving pieces and vases on larger and increasingly elaborate sideboards and tables. The competition to meet these demands drove the furniture industry in America until the second decade of the twentieth century when fashion changes gradually reduced demand and dictated simpler styles.

Many carving details from this special oak furniture are isolated and presented here in photographs to demonstrate the whimsical, elaborate, and intricate work. Today, crafts persons can study these designs and techniques carefully and be inspired by them for their own projects. Through study of the furniture, the ideas of craftsmen of the past can influence the present and future.

The strength that fine oak furniture gives a room is enjoyed by all who live with it every day. They are the people who benefit from the good designs, crisp carving, and ornamental details on fine oak furniture. The ornamental possibilities of carved oak have endeared it to many generations of owners for over a century. Today, when many styles of furniture are available in the competitive marketplace, oak furniture maintains a prominent place because it is solid and strong of function as well as design.

Chapter 1

CASE FURNITURE

A sideboard with finely carved details. The raised backboard has a straight cornice with molded and scroll leaf carved decoration over a plain panel flanked by small lion head carvings. The serving top is rectangular over a long drawer carved with scrolled leaves and punched background. The center of the drawer and tops of the front legs have matching cartouche carvings. The front legs are carved as stylized seated lions on heavy paw feet and are joined horizontally by two rectangular open shelves. 48.25" w. x 47" h. $3000- 4000

Renaissance revival style sideboard with a straight backboard and a wide cornice molding including a charming carved face among gadroons. The rectangular serving shelf overhangs a single drawer with scrolled leaf carving. Turned and ribbed front stiles and back square stiles end in paw feet. The stiles are joined by two rectangular shelves. 50.5" w. x 45.5" h. $2000-2750

Sideboard with serpentine lines dominating the design. The serpentine cornice molding is carved with scrolled leaves, and a narrow shelf at the top over a mirrored back panel is supported by serpentine stiles. The case has a rectangular top which projects at the center over two convex drawers which are flanked by straight cabinet drawers. Below is a long drawer with serpentine skirt supported by front serpentine legs which end in carved paw feet. c. 1900. 41" w. x 57" h. $1100-1250

Sideboard with a raised back board carved at the center top and supporting a shelf on two free-standing cabriole posts above a shaped and beveled mirrored glass panel. The case is bow-shaped with a central drawer, two conforming bowed cabinet doors, and a central rectangular flat door with mirrored glass panel. At the skirt level a long drawer conforms to the shape of the case and has carved leaf accents. The sideboard rests on tall cabriole legs with diamond feet. 39.25" w. x 57.75" h. $1200-1300

Two-part sideboard with exquisite details. The top section has an arched cornice with an applied central carved cartouche with leaf design. An arched frieze is decorated with floral and scrolled leaf carving. The backboard has three rectangular beveled mirrored glass panels in frames behind two projecting side shelves and two boldly turned and reeded posts. The bottom section is a case enclosing two short drawers with scrolled leaf carving, a plain long drawer, and two plain recessed paneled doors separated by a rectangular panel carved with scrolled leaves. The straight base molding rests on carved paw feet. 60" w. x 78.5" h. $5500-6500

One of the finest sideboards of very lively design and exquisite craftsmanship. The backboard is high and arching, with broken pediment and scrolled leaf carving around an oval beveled mirrored glass panel. Two shaped high shelves flank the mirror and are supported by bold s-scrolls carved on the inside and outside surfaces with leaf design. A long shelf is below the mirror and attached to the backboard. The case has a rectangular serving shelf overhanging two short drawers with scrolled leaf carving in a flat area over a plain convex section. Then one plain long drawer rests above two recess paneled doors with carved cartouche and scrolled leaves in the panels. A flat shaped skirt ends the case which rests in ogee paw feet. 49" w. x 70" h. $4000- 4750

Sideboard of Renaissance revival style which retains its original finish. A raised cabinet with carved cornice molding and leaded glass doors is supported over an open shelf and mirrored back panel by carved stiles. The case has two convex drawers over a leaf and scroll carved central panel and two leaded glass doors, and a long convex drawer in the skirt. c. 1890. 46" w. x 72" h. $1500-1850

Opposite: Very nice quality china cabinet and sideboard combination. The left china cabinet has a framed mirrored back above the cabinet with mirrored back, five shelves, and glass door. The right sideboard section has a wooden back over an open shelf and small cabinet enclosed by two leaded glass doors. Below that, a mirrored back panel and open shelf rest above the projecting case where a scrolled drawer and a long drawer rest over two recess paneled cupboard doors. The combined frame rests on four short legs and casters. 72" h. x 44.5" w. $875-1200

Highly unusual three-tiered sideboard. An arched cornice molding is carved with scrolled leaves above a double bowed cabinet with two curved glass side panels and two curved glass front panels. The front panels rest in oak frames hinged as doors and enclose a shelf. At the front corners of the cabinet, two long curved styles protrude, with carvings of scrolled leaves ending in porpoise heads, and rest on smooth round posts that extend in front of the case, two-thirds of the way to its base. A rectangular, beveled mirrored glass panel is framed in the backboard behind an open shelf at the top of the buffet's case. In the case two curved doors flank three short drawers and rest above a long drawer. The plain straight skirt rests on cabriole front legs with leaf carved knees and paw feet. 47.5" h. $3400-3900

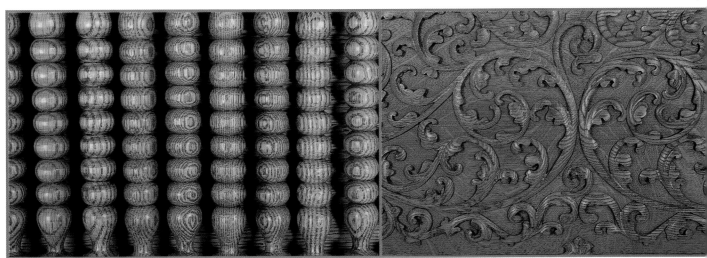

Matching bed and dresser set. The ornate and highly unusual bed frame is distinctive. The high headboard and lower footboard are both curved and serpentine at the top edge and carved throughout with a highly organized scrolling leaf and vine design. Directly below the carving are rows of vertical bead-turned spindles. Below, solid plank panels rest on blocked feet. 64" w.

The dresser has a tilting large beveled mirror in a frame with carving in the cornice matching the head and footboards of the bed. Square posts extending from the top of the dresser support the mirror. The case of the dresser has two small drawers similarly carved over two wide plain drawers, each drawer with scrolled brass pulls and escutcheons. The stiles are carved to match. The case rests on a molded straight base and blocked feet. c. 1880. 84" h. x 60" w.

Matching set of bed, dresser, and wash stand. The bed has a high headboard with symmetrical carved scrolled leaf and blossom design in the cornice which is reinterpreted in the back above the kidney-shaped recessed panel. The same design is repeated in the lower foot board.

The dresser has the same cornice design above the pivoting mirrored glass panel which hangs between carved upright posts. The case has two small over two long drawers, each with brass bail pulls. The case rests on short curved bracket feet. 48" w. x 86" h. The wash stand has a horizontal towel rack on turned upright bars over the case where two long drawers with brass bail pulls rest above two recessed paneled doors. The case rests on short curved bracket feet. 38" w. x 56" h.

Above: Detail of dresser.

Right: Wash stand.

Chest of drawers, also known as a Harlow dresser— named after famed movie actress Jean Harlow who appeared with such furniture in several films. The dominant feature is the pivoting dressing mirror in frame. It is mounted between two stacks of four bowed drawers and above a serpentine long drawer in the base. Plain stiles extend to scrolled feet in the front. 46" w. x 72.5" h. $3500-4000

Tall chest of drawers with carved and turned ornaments. A beveled mirrored glass panel in a shaped and carved frame is adjustable because it is suspended between twist-turned upright posts that are attached to the case of the dresser by a horizontal base. The tall case has a long convex drawer with vertical cuts and applied leaf carving over two small cupboard doors, each with scroll carved recessed panels in plain frames. Then three wide and graduated drawers with brass bail pulls rest between spiral carved stiles above a straight base molding and short bracket feet with casters. 37" w. x 75" h. $2500-3000

Chest of drawers with a raised molding at the back and sides of the rectangular top. The case has four long drawers with brass bail pulls and rests on a straight molded base and short cabriole legs and casters. 26" w. x 30.75" h. $1200-1500

Specialized chest of drawers with combination silver chest and linen press, designed to be efficient. At the top, a shallow case contains twelve drawers arranged in three columns of four drawers each. The projecting deeper case below has a straight molded cornice over two drawers of full width and two stacks of three graduated drawers, each with convex wooden drawer pulls. The straight applied base molding finishes the design. 32" w. x 49" h. $1500-2000

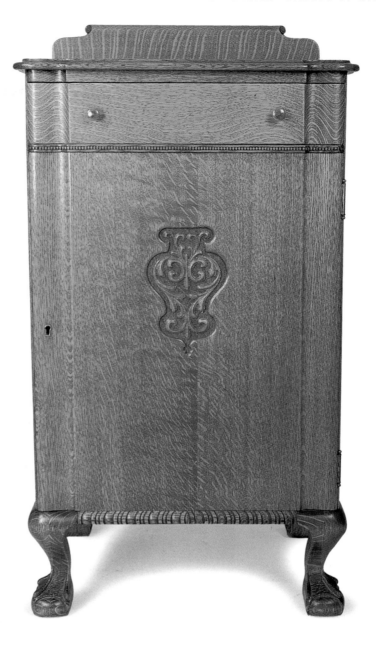

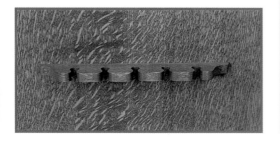

Specialized chest of drawers with cigar and liquor cabinet. A flat backboard with scrolled top is narrower than the case. The rectangular top has a molded edge with inset and rounded front corners overhanging the case of conforming shape. The case has a top drawer and hinged door ornamented with an incised cartouche of punched background and scrolled leaves. Inside, the cabinet is fitted with three compartments, one lined with painted metal sheathing, and the bottom with a stand for nine round glass containers. The straight skirt is lightly gadrooned and rests on short cabriole legs with square paw feet. 22.25" w. x 42.5" h. No price available

One of a pair of exceptional and rare corner cupboards in two parts. The straight, dentiled, and concave cornice overhangs a frieze incised with s-scrolls. The top section has two rectangular doors with plain glass panels and applied fretwork at the top enclosing four shelves. The bottom section has a long drawer an applied carved shell pull and scrolled leaves, and two recess paneled doors, each with an applied carved animal head, floral, and scrolled leaf decoration. The off-set corners of both cases have twist-turned columns and the molded base has ogee bracket feet with off-set corners. 41" w. x 86" h. No price available

Large and very unusual corner cupboard with a straight cornice molding overhanging the top case that has two flat doors with beveled glass enclosing three shelves. At the center, an open shelf has beveled mirrored glass back panels and free-standing turned corner posts. The lower case has a single long drawer and two recessed paneled doors with carved leaf and floral design. The straight applied base molding extends to the floor. 41.5" w. x 83.5" h. $4500-5000

Solid roll-top desk with horizontal slats enclosing the
writing surface and interior compartments. The case has
two matching stacks of four drawers and a long center
drawer above the open knee hole. The case rests on an
applied base molding. 50" w. x 51.5" h. $2800-3400

Kidney shaped desk with conforming top and case. A central drawer is flanked by two cases of four stacked drawers, each with veneered scroll leaf carved fronts and shell designed pulls. The case rests on paw feet. 51.25" w. $4200-5000.

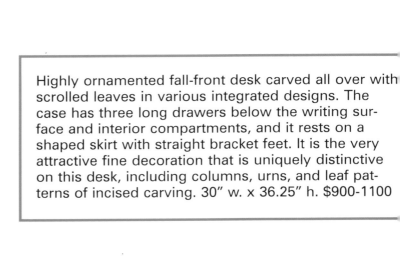

Highly ornamented fall-front desk carved all over with scrolled leaves in various integrated designs. The case has three long drawers below the writing surface and interior compartments, and it rests on a shaped skirt with straight bracket feet. It is the very attractive fine decoration that is uniquely distinctive on this desk, including columns, urns, and leaf patterns of incised carving. 30" w. x 36.25" h. $900-1100

Fall-front desk on legs with an unusual amount of carved detail. The top has a shaped and scroll-carved backboard. The case has a straight molding and matched flame grain wood in the hinged fall front writing surface. Inside, small compartments and two drawers are carefully fitted. A long drawer below the writing surface has applied long c-scrolls and leaf scroll carving. Below that drawer inset lion head carvings flank a deep shaped drawer which has a central cartouche and leaf carving. The case is supported by tall leaf-carved cabriole legs with paw feet. Unusual to this desk are a fully finished oak back surface and fully carved back legs. 37.25" w. x 47" h. $3500-4200

Very pretty and unusual combination book-case and lady's fall-front desk. At the top, an oval mirrored glass panel in frame is flanked by two shaped panels, each bearing floral carvings and a small projecting shelf with pierced brackets and a turned support. On each side of the desk, a rounded case has a curved glass door enclosing a shelf over a curved drawer and thin square cabriole legs joined front to back with shaped rectangular shelves and top to bottom with two turned posts. In the center, the fall-front desk with applied floral garland carving rests over a long straight drawer and a pierced stretcher joining the backs of the side shelves. 44" w. x 62.25" h. $4500-5200

Wildly undulating bookcase and fall-front desk of large size and unusually fine design. A flat backboard supports applied carving in urn and scroll design. The serpentine bookcase on the left has two curved glass doors enclosing shelves above an open conforming wooden shelf. The straight desk on the right has a shaped mirrored glass back panel over a pillow drawer, fall-front writing surface, and three straight drawers, each part with applied symmetric scroll carving. The base rests on short cabriole legs. c. 1890. 49.5" w. x 68.75" h. No price available

Elegant cylinder desk with bookcase, or secretary, with a broad cornice bearing egg and dart molding over a frieze with ribbon and floral garland carving. Two glazed doors in the bookcase section enclose three oak shelves. The desk's cylinder cover for the writing surface has two recessed panels each carved with scrolled leaf design. A long drawer with applied rectangular sections rests over two plain drawers and a door with a recessed panel containing lively symmetric scrolled leaf and berry carving. c. 1880. 45.75" w. x 95.5" h. $8000-9000

Very nice quality combination bookcase and desk. A projecting straight cornice is supported by two lion mask carvings on posts in front of two beveled and mirrored glass panels. The bookcase on the left side has a curved front with plain top molding over glass paneled door enclosing five shelves. To the right, a long convex drawer rests over the fall-front desk with hinged flap bearing applied animal mask, c-scroll, and leaf carving. Below the writing surface the case is deeply convex in the area where three drawers gradually change in contour and rest on a straight base molding and three carved paw front feet. 44.25" w. x 77.5" h. $2800-3300

Attractive bookcase and desk with fine quality applied carving to the shaped tops and mirrored back panels of both the bookcase and desk sections. Two candle arms swing out over the long drawer and leaf carved writing surface of the fall front desk and three slightly convex drawers. The bookcase has a convex glass door enclosing five conforming shelves. The curved base rests on short cabriole legs and carved paw feet. c. 1900. 44.5" w. x 76" h. $5200-6000

Quite an interesting and beautiful Art Nouveau style combination bookcase and desk. The backboard extends above the case and is pierced with an asymmetrical carved leaf design at the center and faced with a beveled mirrored glass panel with curved corners in a conforming frame. A shelf, part straight and part curved, is supported above the case with two carved figures as supports, one a short-necked griffin (at the left) and the other a long-necked griffin (at the right). The case has a bookcase on the left with a curved glass door enclosing five shelves. At the right, an arched and beveled glass panel rests above a fall-front desk with applied scroll carving on the writing surface flap. The desk has a convex long drawer over two flat long drawers, each with brass bail pulls. The case rests on short cabriole legs. 39" w. x 74.75" h. No price available

Strongly figured, quarter-sawed wood is featured in this finely designed combination bookcase and desk. The backboard extends far above the case with a carved cornice of symmetrical scrolled leaf carving. A rounded frieze rests over two rectangular beveled and mirrored glass panels with top corners that are curved inward. Two side shelves curve to form a canopy over the open shelf over the case and are supported by delicately turned bulbous posts. The left side of the case has a straight rectangular bookcase with a flat glass-paneled door enclosing five shelves. The right side of the case has a fall-front desk with a narrow shelf and convex long drawer over the hinged flap. Inside, open shelves, letter slots, and two small drawers are built above the writing surface. The case has a serpentine-shaped drawer over two flat drawers and rests on carved paw feet. 45.25" w. x 79" h. $3500-4000

Chapter 2
BOOKCASES

Bookcase that is quite charming in its simplicity. The only ornamentation are carved sea horses at the top of the flat door with glass panel. The case encloses four shelves and rests on undeveloped paw feet. 29" w. x 61" h. $1200-1500

Nice bookcase which has an egg-and-dart molding in the cornice. The straight door has applied scroll carving at the top and a glass panel enclosing five shelves. The shaped base molding rests on cabriole legs and casters. 32" w. x 67.5" h. $2200-2600

Left: Bookcase with a shaped and beveled glass back panel above the case where glass shelves are enclosed by the glass door. The case has a single drawer in the base with nicely shaped lower edge and carved center. The piece rests on short cabriole legs. 74" h. x 24.5" w. No price available

Right: Interesting bookcase with a raised back that includes pierced and shaped elements around an open shelf. The straight case has a glass paneled door enclosing four shelves and it rests on short bracket feet. 24.5" w. x 61" h. $1000-1400

Opposite: Bookcase with straight cornice molding and two arched panel doors with glass panes divided by wooden mullions. The case encloses six shelves and rests on a straight base molding and short cabriole feet. 47" w. x 70.75" h. $3200-3500

Below: Double bookcase with straight cornice molding over an applied scrolled leaf carved frieze. The stiles have ionic capitals over the same applied leaf carving and a lower reeded rectangular section with blocked feet. The straight doors have glass panels in plain frames enclosing five shelves. 57" w. x 66" h. $3500-3900

Excellent quality Eastlake style bookcase with straight gallery at the top and carved molding over reeded and fluted stiles. The flat glazed doors and four interior shelves are over two drawers of hand-cut dovetailed construction. c. 1870. 51.25" w. x 86" h. $3200-3775

Left: Double door bookcase with a raised back ornamented at the center with scroll, face and leaf carving. A round cornice with carved ends overhangs the case where two flat glass panels in plain frames are hinged to enclose five shelves. The straight base molding rests on carved paw feet. 46.25" w. x 67" h. No price available

ight: Fine bookcase with a raised back ornamented at the center with an asymmetrical cartouche and leaf carving and with metal rails at the sides of the rectangular top. An open shelf area has shaped side brackets carved with scrolled leaves and a rectangular mirrored glass panel at the back. The case has two flat glass panels in plain frames as doors hinged to enclose four shelves. A straight base molding has incised carving on the skirt and short bracket feet. 37" w. x 67" h. $2200-2500

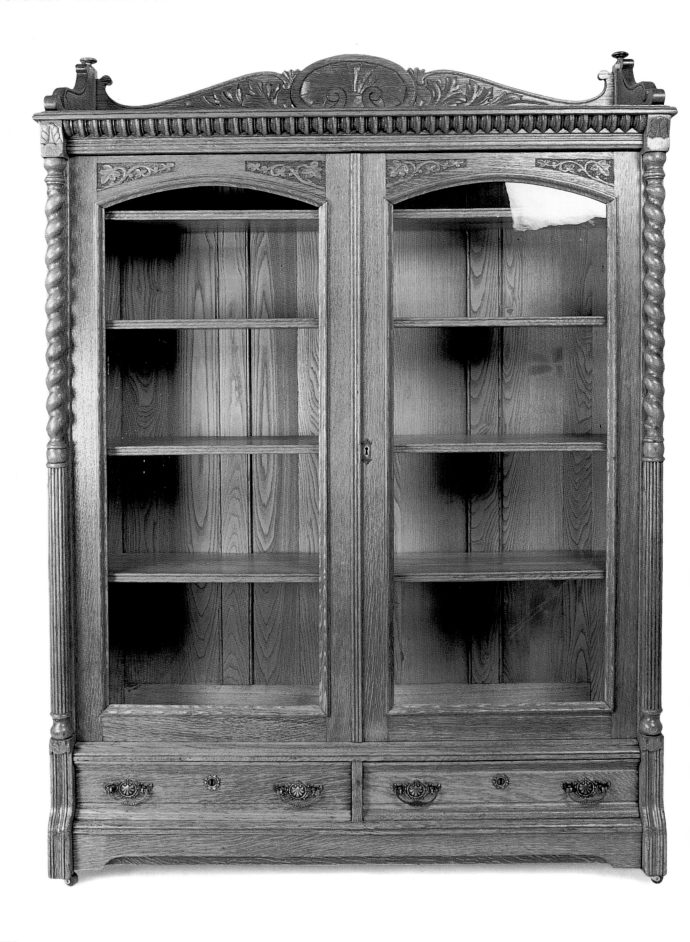

Bookcase of very pleasant character. The backboard is arched with shell and scrolled leaf carving and it curls to meet the curving side rails at the back corners. The case has a straight top with spool-turned molding. The stiles are carved with twists above reeded sections and bulbous ends. Two flat doors with leaf and punched decoration in the curving top frame have glass panels and enclose five shelves. Two short drawers in the base molding have brass bail pulls. 50" w. x 71" h. No price available

Above: Triple door bookcase with rounded corners and direct carving details. The straight cornice molding is gadrooned over the case where three straight glass panels are hinged as doors. Each door encloses four shelves with applied rope-carved front edges. The case rests on a gadrooned base and short ogee feet with casters. 64" w/ x 57" h. $2800-3200

Opposite: Magnificent triple door bookcase of impressive design and size. Two flat bookcases flank the central curved bookcase and all are contained within a strong frame and divided by rope twist carved pillars. The cornice is molded, gadrooned, and conforming with the case by projecting at the center. A frieze is beautifully carved with mask and scrolled leaf design above the glass doors. Each case has five separate shelves. The base molding is stepped and gadrooned and rests on four front and two back short cabriole legs. 74" w. x 69" h. $7000-8000

Stacked bookcases were first produced c. 1883 by the Globe Warneke Company in Cincinnati, Ohio.

5-level stacking bookcase, unusual with its raised paneled ends. The case is plain with gently shaped stiles including brass bands where the levels attach. Each bookshelf has a sliding door with straight glass front and brass knob pull. A slightly raised base molding completes the design. 36" w. x 71" h. $2000-2500

Top: Unusual double-wide, quarter-sawed oak bookcase of three vertical sections. This heavy bookcase is dated 1899 on the back panel and labeled by the Gunn Manufacturing Company of Grand Rapids, Michigan. 50.5" w. x 50.25" h. $1500-1795

Bottom: Bookcase of unusual construction with three glass-enclosed sections above three file drawers. c. 1900. 42" w. x 66" h. $2200-2650

CHAIRS

Heavily carved side chair with a solid, mushroom-shaped back. The back carving of two winged animals with lion heads tied together at the necks has a contrasting dark and roughened background. The round seat has a leather upholstery and rests on four turned legs joined by a turned H-stretcher. No price available

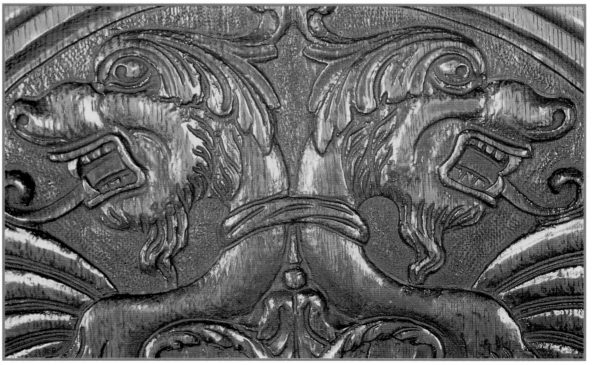

Above: Drafting stoo[l] with a deep and curved tapering back[ ]support on rectangu[lar] stiles. The rounded seat swivels on an ir[on] joint over a four-legged flaring base with ring foot rest an[d] applied bracing. 43" $700-800

Left: Windsor side chair with a curved crest and spool turne[d] spindles and bracing spindles. The plank seat is shaped and rounded and rests o[n] four raking turned le[gs] joined by a turned H stretcher. $500-600

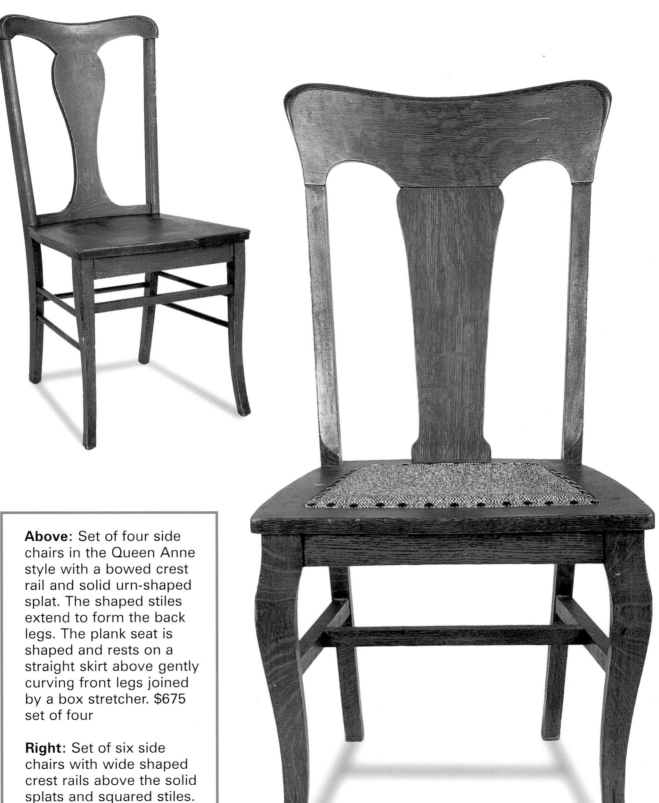

Above: Set of four side chairs in the Queen Anne style with a bowed crest rail and solid urn-shaped splat. The shaped stiles extend to form the back legs. The plank seat is shaped and rests on a straight skirt above gently curving front legs joined by a box stretcher. $675 set of four

Right: Set of six side chairs with wide shaped crest rails above the solid splats and squared stiles. The seats are upholstered inside the frame and rest on cabriole legs joined by an H-stretcher and claw feet. $1450-1600 set of six

Set of eight Chippendale style chairs comprising two arm and six side chairs. The serpentine crest rails rest on pierced Gothic splats and tapering stiles. The seats are upholstered inside the slip seats and straight frames on cabriole legs joined by an H-stretcher and ball and claw feet. $3500-4500 set of two arm and six side

Set of one arm chair and five side chairs in the Renaissance revival style with deeply carved crest rails of a symmetrical cartouche, scrolled leaf, and berry design. The rectangular back panels and seats are upholstered and attached inside a beaded oak frame. The arms curve downward and end in tight scrolls above urn-turned and reeded supports. The back legs are rectangular extensions of the back stiles, and are joined to the turned and reeded front legs by H-shaped stretchers above the carved feet. $4500-4800 set of one arm and five side

Right: Arm chair with turned balls and spindles in the solid frame. The back and seat are cushioned with a long tufted pillow which extends from the crest rail to the front seat rail. The frame rests on a shaped skirt with medallion carving and square cabriole front legs. $800-950

Left: Set of six formal ladder back side chairs with four curved and bowed slats between the raking stiles. The seat is upholstered within the frame and shaped skirt. Cabriole front legs are joined by a box stretcher. $1100-1400 set of six

Office arm chair with a deep and scrolling head rest over an upholstered black leather rectangular back and seat. The arms curve and flare with scrolled knuckles over a square curving arm supports and a straight wooden skirt. The seat swivels in an iron joint above four flat curving legs and casters. 44" h. $700-850

Continuous arm "lollipop" arm chair by George Hunzinger Company of New York. The graduated spindles end in flat and round turnings above a seat upholstered within the bowed frame and resting on splayed back legs and curved front legs. c. 1880. 34.5" h. $1200-1400.

Platform rocking arm chair made by the Geo[r] Hunzinger Company of New York, with The Hunzinger Duplex Spri[n] patented Sept. 26, 188[2] paper label on the seat frame advises: "One dr[op] of oil from your sewing machine can, on every joint of hinge, will preve[nt] noise." The curved bac[k] is comprised of turned spindles. Short turned spindles are arranged i[n] curves to form the arm[s] with the front posts topped by ball turnings The seat is upholstered with black leather tacke[d] within the frame and re[st] on a ribbed skirt and th[e] duplex spring mecha-nism. No price availabl[e]

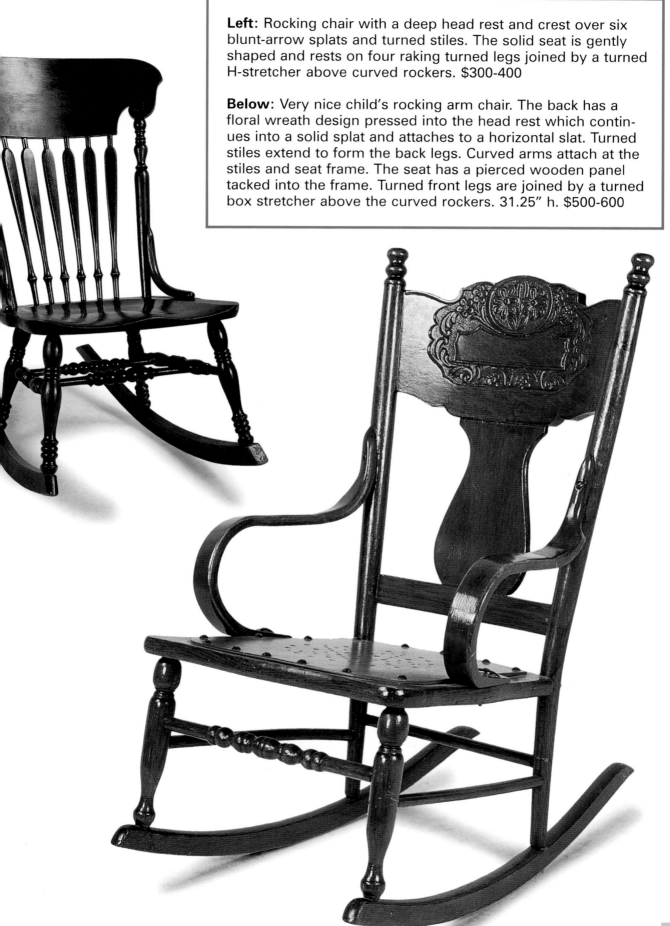

Left: Rocking chair with a deep head rest and crest over six blunt-arrow splats and turned stiles. The solid seat is gently shaped and rests on four raking turned legs joined by a turned H-stretcher above curved rockers. $300-400

Below: Very nice child's rocking arm chair. The back has a floral wreath design pressed into the head rest which continues into a solid splat and attaches to a horizontal slat. Turned stiles extend to form the back legs. Curved arms attach at the stiles and seat frame. The seat has a pierced wooden panel tacked into the frame. Turned front legs are joined by a turned box stretcher above the curved rockers. 31.25" h. $500-600

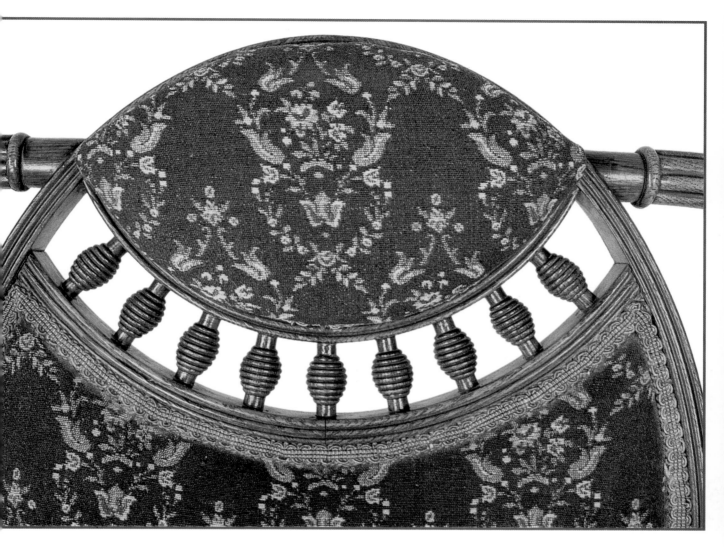

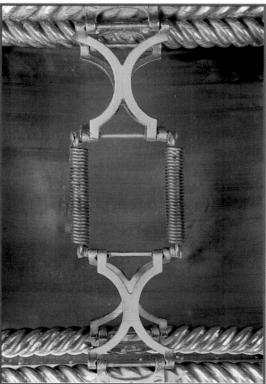

Platform rocking chair made by the George Hunzinger Company of New York. An upholstered oval back panel is interrupted with nine bulbous spindle turned posts in a ribbed frame. The back is supported with a curving, round, and ribbed crest rail, twist turned stiles, and five plain posts. The flat arms have rectangular upholstered pads, double-u-shaped sides, and twist-turned supports. The rectangular upholstered seat rests in a straight skirt above the patented duplex spring mechanism and rectangular platform frame. c. 1880. 40.5" h. No price available

Rocking arm chair. The frame of the curving back is carved with an elaborate open design of dolphins, bell flowers, and curving leaves. The conforming solid back panel is oak with an inscribed c-scroll at the top. Flat arms curve forward with three small flat cabriole-shaped supports and a larger conforming end that supports scrolled knuckles. The dished seat is supported by cabriole front legs, a turned H-stretcher and back legs, and curved rockers. c. 1880. No price available

Ingeniously-designed child's adjustable chair that can be set in four positions: as a high chair, youth chair, stroller, and rocking chair. The back and seat are filled with woven cane. The solid wooden tray is hinged to be forward when in use or swing behind when not needed. The interesting support mechanism varies the positions of the legs and iron wheels serve as feet. c. 1900. $900-1100

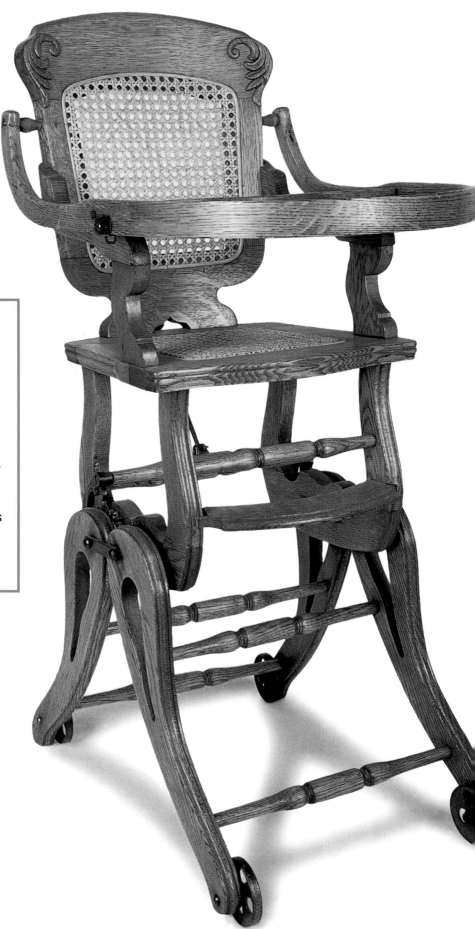

Hall chair of wide design with curving leaves carved at the crest of the thickly framed back. A flat urn-shaped splat is pierced with five vertical slits. Straight arms rest on three turned spindles above a flat seat hinged to conceal a compartment below. Flat and shaped arm supports continue down to form the splayed legs between which the deep skirt has an applied leaf carving and serpentine bottom edge. 24″ w. x 36″ h. No price available

A bench with elaborate carving and a storage compartment under the seat. This useful and attractive furniture has a rectangular back panel with symmetrical leaf scroll carving in a wide frame around the central raised panel. The stiles extend above the back with leaf carving and paneled space above the attached arms. The straight arms flare to curved knuckles above the cyma curved supports. The seat of the bench is hinged at the back and encloses a storage compartment behind the deep skirt which is decorated with a raised panel and two carved ovoid panels. The square front legs are channel carved and end in paw feet. 50"w. x 44"h. $2700-3000

Fine Windsor style bench with high relief shell, scroll, and leaf carved crest and ten spindles in the curved back, plank seat, turned stiles, arms with scrolled knuckles, and turned legs joined by an H-stretcher. The back spindles are unevenly spaced on this bench, and that is how it came from the factory.

Careful observation shows no repairs or alternate holes in the crest to receive the spindles, but the third spindle from the right (see detail) is spaced closer to its left neighbor than the other spindles. c. 1880. 42" w. x 33" h. $1800-2175

Elegant Chippendale style bench with serpentine crest hand carved with a central cartouche and scrolled leaves over three solid vase shaped splats, plank seat, arms with scrolled knuckles on serpentine supports, skirt serpentine shaped, raking back legs and serpentine front legs joined by H-stretchers and ending in carved paw feet. c. 1880. 45.5" w. x 38.5" h. $1800-2250

Very rare tête-à-tête love seat with two opposing seats in a common frame. Each side has a pierced and upholstered chair back with scenic tapestry covering above a lyre-shaped carved wooden section with scrolled leaves design. The two seats are both shaped on a continuous plank supported by four turned legs that are joined by a turned H-stretcher. Turned spindles join the curving arms with the seat. 42.25" w. $2100-2400

Chapter 4
CHINA CABINETS

Small china cabinet by Flint Manufacturing Company of Grand Rapids, Michigan, and sold by John Wanamaker stores in Philadelphia, New York, and Paris. Three curved sides and a conforming case have a molded cornice over a plain frieze. The sides and hinged door each contain large rounded glass panels and enclose adjustable shelves and a mirrored back. The conforming base molding is serpentine in the front and rests on tall cabriole legs that end in paw feet. 32" w. x 51" h. $2400-2600

Large curio cabinet by Flint Manufacturing Company of Grand Rapids, Michigan. Three curved sides and a conforming case have a molded and gadrooned cornice over a carved frieze. The sides and hinged door each contain large rounded glass panels and enclose adjustable shelves and a mirrored back. The conforming base molding is serpentine in the front and rests on tall cabriole legs that end in paw feet. 38.25" w. x 82.5" h. $3400-3600

Left: Curio cabinet by Flint Manufacturing Company of Grand Rapids, Michigan. Three curved sides and a conforming case have a molded and gadrooned cornice over a convex frieze. The sides and hinged door each contain large curved glass panels and enclose four adjustable shelves and a mirrored back. Stiles have leaf carving at the tops. The conforming base molding is serpentine with incised carving in the front and the case rests on tall cabriole legs that end in paw feet. 36" w. x 60.5" h. $3000-3400

Right: China cabinet of large and impressive size. The straight cornice molding overhangs a frieze carved in the center with a medallion and scrolled leaves. The case has curved sides and serpentine front, with conforming glass panels in frames enclosing five shelves and a mirrored back. The conforming base molding rests on four cabriole legs with paw feet. 44" w. x 67.5" h. $3600-3800.

Opposite: China cabinet with a pagoda-like personality. The backboard that extends ab[...] the case is shaped high at the center with l[...] c-scrolls and flares at the curving ends. The case has a deep stepped molding above tw[...] curved glass side panels and a straight glas[...] front panel that is framed and hinged as a d[...] all enclosing glass shelves. The skirt is carv[...] with c-scrolls and rests on tall scrolled legs [...] paw feet. 35.25" w. x 57" h. $2600-2900

Very elaborately carved china cabinet in a style usually made in mahogany and very rare in oak. It was made by the Edinburgh Cabinet Company of Edinburgh, Indiana, successors to the C. Blake Furniture Company and C. F. W. Schlimper & Co. of Boston, Massachusetts. The most outstanding features are the large and fancy scroll, leaf, and floral carving at the top of the case, and the carved frame around the side and front glass panels. The rectangular case has a hinged door enclosing four shelves and it rests on cabriole legs that end in scrolled feet. c. 1890. 36.25" w. x 76" h. $4800-5000

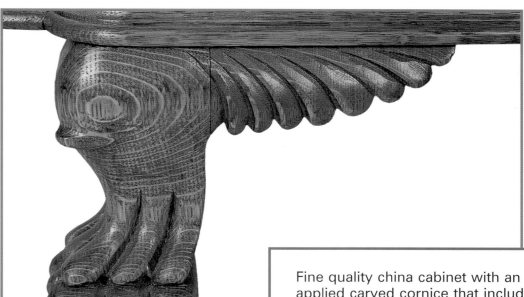

Fine quality china cabinet with an unusual applied carved cornice that includes animal heads, scrolled leaves and nuts in a symmetrical design. The case is curved at the sides and flat in front with conforming glass panels, the center one hinged as a door between reeded and turned stiles. The case encloses adjustable shelves and rests on a plain base molding and unusual bracket feet, finely carved as winged paws. 49" w. x 69" h. $4800-5200

Marvelous china cabinet with rounded sides and straight front. The cornice has a projecting central carving of c-scrolls and leaves in an architectural frame with punched background. The case has matching glass panels on the three sides, including top sections of leaded shield-shaped panels above plain bottom sections. The case encloses a mirrored back at the top and four shelves and rests on a plain base molding and small carved paw feet. 34.75" w. x 67" h. No price available

Right: Very tall half-round, two-part china cabinet of unusual design. This commanding piece has a wide frieze beautifully carved and punched with a scroll design and two rope twist vertical columns at the front of both sections. The mirrored back of the case and six shelves in all are enclosed by convex glass doors. The shaped skirt has carving on three sides and rests on two ball and claw carved front feet and two square blocked back feet. c. 1880. 40" w. x 90.5" h. $12,000-15,000

Opposite: Half round china cabinet with a straight convex frieze. The case has three curved glass panels separated by two half round stiles carved at the tops and bottoms with scrolled leaves. The central panel is a hinged door that encloses mirrored back at the top and five shelves. The straight conforming base rests on square paw feet. 47" w. x 72" h. $4500-4900

Monumental china cabinet with serpentine front and two curved sides. The flat cornice molding and convex frieze conform to the shape of the cabinet with boldly stepped, scrolled leaf carved, flat plinths flanking the curved center. Curved glass front and side panels enclose four interior shelves and the mirrored glass backboard. The stiles are boldly carved with standing lions on blocked plinths and geometric carved pedestals. The stepped base molding rests on carved vigorous paw feet. 53.75" w. x 70.75" h. No price available

Details of previuos cabinet

China cabinet of fine, tall proportion with mirrored back and open shelf over four interior shelves. The case is in desirable original finish and has curved side glass over the oval base on scrolled legs with casters. c. 1900. 42.5" w. x 78" h. $3000-3275

China cabinet of unusually large size and interesting design. The backboard extends above the case with a central leaf carving and turtle-shaped, beveled mirrored glass panel in frame. Flanking the mirror are two flat and gadrooned sections, each with a shaped shelf, pierced leaf carving, and turned and scalloped supporting post. The case has curved sides and a flat center with conforming glass panels in frames enclosing four shelves. The flat door in the center is shorter than the sides and rests above a single drawer in the molded base. Small paw feet carry the case. 48" w. x 72" h. $4300-4800

Magnificent architectural china cabinet. The case has a molded cornice carved at the center with an amusing animal face and scrolled leaf design. The cornice conforms to the case with curved sides and a straight front. An open shelf with an oval beveled mirrored glass panel in the backboard has two carved griffin-head and leaf design posts supporting the cornice in the front. The projecting case has glass panels in the curved sides and flat front enclosing five shelves. Rope-twist carved stiles extend to the base molding and paw feet on casters. 49.5" w. x 76" h. $9500-10,000

Left: China cabinet with classic, uncluttered lines and elegant proportions. The back of the cabinet extends above the case with an oval beveled glass panel in a plain frame. The oval case has three curved glass panels in plain frames. The central panel is hinged as a door between round stiles. The case rests on four tall legs with paw carved feet. 32" w. x 64" h. $2500-2800

Right: China cabinet of oval shape with molded cornice and central carved floral decoration. The canopy has two lion head carvings in the frieze over cabriole posts and a beveled mirrored glass panel in the backboard. The case has curved sides and front with glass panels in plain frames enclosed in a mirrored glass back at the top and five shelves. The round stiles extend to a molded base, short cabriole legs, and carved paw feet. 40" w. x 75" h. $5000-5500

Monumental china cabinet of exceptional design and size. The shaped cornice molding rests above a mirrored back and free-standing griffin and grape carvings that enclose an open shelf. Below, the case conforms to the shape of the cornice and has a lovely leaf carved frieze and lion head capitals to the two major supports. The case extends down with three curved glass panels, the center one in a hinged door frame, enclosing four shelves. The conforming base molding rests on boldly carved paw feet. c. 1890. 50.5" w. x 74" h. $12,000-14000

Details of previous cabinet.

Chapter 5
TABLES

Hastings & Brown of Hastings, Michigan,
made tables of especially good quality.

DINING TABLES

Rectangular extension dining table with a thick 48" wide
and long top and four additional leaves, each 12" wide, to
extend the length to eight feet. The skirt has a repeating
geometric frieze and gadrooned edge. Six bold and tapering
turned legs have carved onion turnings above reeding,
spool turnings, and brass casters. c. 1890. $2500-2800

Fine round dining table by Horner, New York. The 60" diameter top has two half-round ends with four leaves, each of 12" width, to expand the top to nine feet. The skirt is carved with four rectangular sections of scrolled leaf and punched decoration. The round pedestal support and four magnificent, free-standing griffin carvings rest on a platform with four extensions and carved paw feet. c. 1890. $15,000-16,000.

Details of previous
dining table.

Wonderful rectangular Italian Renaissance revival library table with a plain top and incised molded edge overhanging the skirt. The convex skirt comprises a heavily carved frieze of c-scrolls and shells design including two drawers separated by a prominent leaf carving. The table rests on two large and bulbous turned end posts and five lesser turned and leaf carved center posts above a molded stretcher and stepped platform feet. 64" w. x 22.25" d. x 28.5" h. $3300-3500

Details of previous table.

This highly unusual library table by Horner, New York, is finished on four sides with a rectangular top carved with a border of scrolled leaves. Two pillow drawers in the skirt have vertical carving and brass bail pulls. The most unusual feature is the use of back-to-back griffin carved side supports which make a dramatic presence. The carving is elaborate and shallow with the scrolled leaf design of the top carving reflected in the hair of the beasts. A flat stretcher shelf with gadrooned edge rests on horizontal platforms with scroll carved ends and castors. c. 1890. 54" w. x 30.5" h. x 32" d. $6200-6500

Details of previous table.

Rectangular library table with rounded and serpentine corners overhanging the skirt. A single drawer with leaf carved and s-curved front edge has two brass bail pulls and back plates. The turned legs are reeded above the stretcher shelf and taper to end in bulbous feet. 36" w. x 30.25" h. x 25.75" d. $1200-1500

An unusual library table with a rectangular top with molded edge and cut corners overhanging the skirt. Two drawers in the skirt have brass bail handles and the skirt has both central and side brackets with incised carving. The table rests on four turned legs joined by a rectangular shelf with pierced front and back gallery. 38" w. x 27" d. $1200-1500

Unusual and interesting games table with a four-lobed swivel top that pivots to expose four wells for chips or counters. An original dark finish is a nice authentic feature. The four legs curve inward to support a four-lobed shelf and flare out at the feet. 28" square. $1200-1400

Rectangular center table with a molded top over-hanging an incised skirt with applied drapery pieces at the lower edge. Four turned legs are joined by a rectangular shelf with gadrooned edge and end in turned feet with casters. 30" w. x 22" d. $1000-1200

Left: Center table with a shaped and rounded top overhanging a square frame. Its four legs have turned and flat pierced sections and are joined by a four-sided shelf. The legs splay out above the paw carved feet. 24" h. $800-900

Right: Center table with rectangular top cut out at the edges with symmetrical scallops. Four turned and reeded posts are joined by a rectangular shelf also cut out at the edges with scallops. The four serpentine curved legs have leaf carvings at the top and end in scrolled feet. 24" h. $800-900

Left: Three-sided center table with three-lobed top supported by three turned and reeded supports. A three-lobed shelf joins the supports above three round and flaring legs. 26" w. $800-900

Right: Square center table with molded edge and inset curved corners over-hanging the conforming skirt. The top rests on four sausage-turned legs joined by a shelf with curved cut-outs. The legs end with claw talons and glass ball feet. 27.5" square. $800-900

Square center table with a molded edge overhanging the skirt that has incised carving and turned drops at the four corners. Four turned posts support the top and are flanking a bowl-shaped turning that rests on a central plinth. Four c-shaped flat legs with incised carving and turned drops end in turned bun feet. 21.5" square. $1100-1250

Rectangular table made by George Hunzinger Company of New York. The top of the table is a rectangular beveled glass panel set into a carved frame with gadrooned edge that overhangs four tightly turned legs with brass ends and paw feet.

Between the legs are two sets of turned stretchers that join with a rectangular box on its side. The box is made up of four panels of twist-turned and interwoven carved oak spindles. 32.25" w. x 28" h. No price available

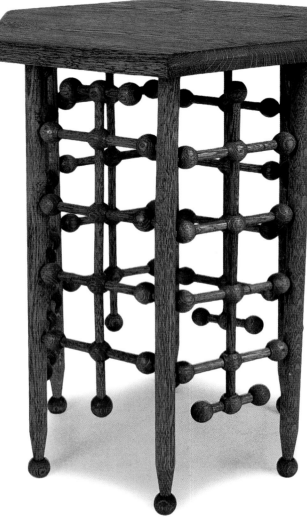

Left: Center table with a brass ring supported on four brass plinths above the round oak top. The top has a molded edge overhanging four legs with deep s-curve profile that are joined by a round shelf. 15.5" d. x 21.5" h. No price available

Right: Six-sided "tabaret stand" center table with a plank top with molded edge overhanging six legs that are joined by stick and ball turnings. The legs end in ball feet. 14" w. x 19" h. $300-400

Pair of elegant plant stands with round, flat tops molded at the edges and resting on tall turned stems with reeded necks and cross-hatched urns. Narrow turned plinths rest on flat round bases and four carved feet. 13.25" d. x 45" h. $1000-1100 pair

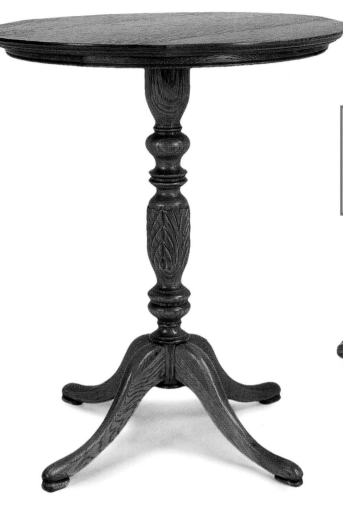

Left: Pedestal table with a gently shaped, nearly round top overhanging the turned pedestal stem and four raking legs. 24" d. $800-900

Right: Rectangular pedestal table with square flat top beaded at the lower edge. The top rests on a pedestal with four turnings above a square plinth, four flat incised panels, and a tapering end. A stepped platform base has a gadrooned edge above four flaring paw feet. 17" square. $700-800

Chapter 6
ACCENT PIECES

Shaving stand with an oval mirrored glass panel in plain frame suspended by two curving arms over the case. A rectangular shelf with molded edge overhangs a serpentine drawer, rounded stiles, and a rectangular shelf over two serpentine drawers, the bottom edge of the lower one with a conforming curved skirt. The case rests on cabriole legs. 22.25" w. x 68" h. No price available

Shaving stand with an oval mirrored glass panel in plain frame mounted on an iron adjustable frame. The case has a rectangular top over a long drawer and two doors, one being flat and the other serpentine. The case is supported by flat shaped side pieces joined by an oval and a rectangular shelf and four flat cabriole legs. 14" w. x 64" h. $2000-2200

Shaving stand #4879 labeled by Paine Furniture Company of Boston, Massachusetts. This truly elegant piece has a beveled mirrored glass panel in plain frame suspended by two curving arms above the case. Two small drawers and a projecting shelf rest over three long bowed drawers upon four tall and thin cabriole legs joined by a rectangular shelf. 19" w. x 70" h. No price available

Shaving stand with a rectangular and concave-sided beveled mirrored glass panel in plain frame mounted on a turned post over the case. A rectangular shelf with serpentine front edge overhangs a conforming drawer and sides that become pierced and bend inward below the drawer. The pierced sides attach to a square block with molded edges. The block rests on a round reeded column above a round base, rectangular platform with concave sides, and four carved paw feet. 65" h. No price available

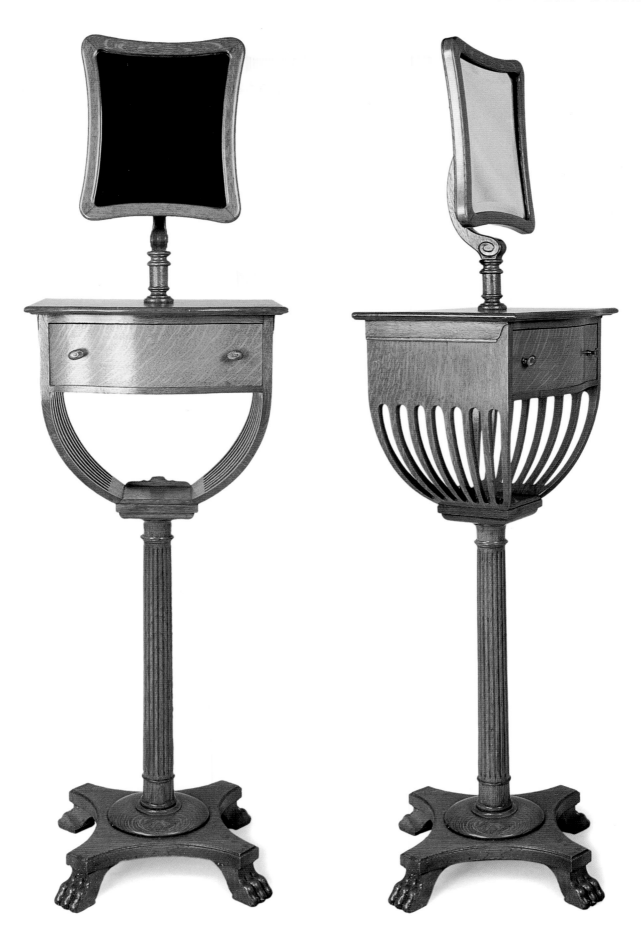

DRESSING GLASS

Dressing glass in a plain rectangular frame. The mirrored glass panel is supported by a stand with a straight cornice and lovely leaf-carved frieze. Turned side supports are fluted, and where the looking glass supports join the frame the blocks are carved with a floral blossom. The fluted legs of the stand curve to the front and back and rest on casters. 34" w. x 80" h. $2400-2600

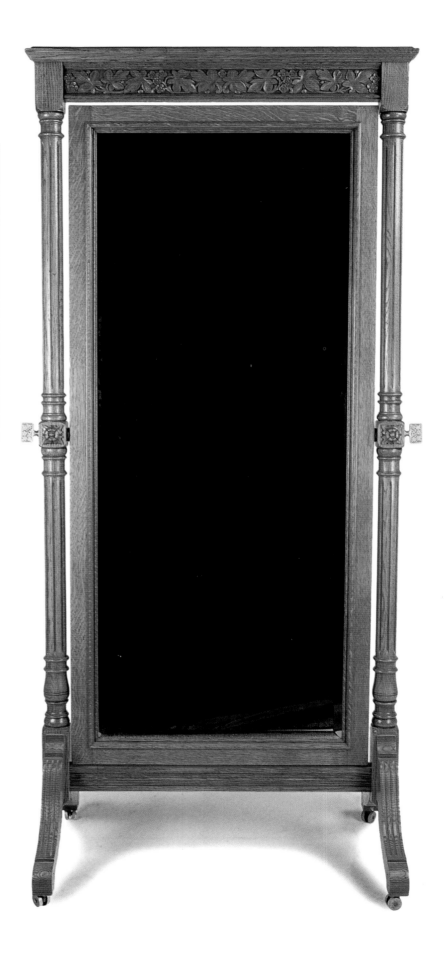

Quite a tall hall stand with cornice carved as a central fan flanked by opposing lion-headed scrolls. The straight cornice overhangs an open frieze composed of turned and post and ball elements. In the main section, six small beveled rectangular glass "derby" mirrors with leaded frames are tilted down in a frame above the long rectangular looking glass. The stiles are carved with rope twist and flower elements. The base section has three red marble panels on a shelf above openwork carving, turned posts, and a plain curved base molding. 33" w. x 94" h. $3800-4000

Hall stand with a large mirrored glass panel in the back. The frame is ornamented with scroll, shell, and floral carving and four double butterfly metal hat hooks. A projecting storage case has a hinged lid and flanking side compartments, all resting on flat bracket feet with c-scroll outlines. 48" w. x 88" h. $5600-6000

Hall stand with a tall backboard carved at the top with an applied c-scroll and leaf design. A beveled mirrored glass panel is set into a deep frame with more applied leaf and c-scroll carving at the bottom. Four double hooks of cast metal with lion head designs are attached to the backboard. The stand has a base of chair form with brass umbrella ring attached, flat curving arms, and deeply serpentine front legs with paw feet. The seat area is hinged to contain a compartment in the deep skirt. 40" w. x 84" h. $4000-4400

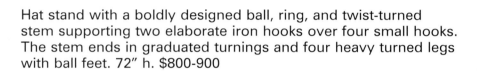

Hat stand with a boldly designed ball, ring, and twist-turned stem supporting two elaborate iron hooks over four small hooks. The stem ends in graduated turnings and four heavy turned legs with ball feet. 72" h. $800-900

Left: Hat stand with a nicely turned stem supporting three metal s-hooks and four turned short posts before it rests on four turned splayed legs. 69.5″ h. $ 400-500

Right and details: Hat stand with a boldly turned and leaf carved stem supporting iron s-hooks and four short iron hooks. The stem rests on four raking curved legs carved with leaf design and carved paw feet. 78.5″ h. No price available

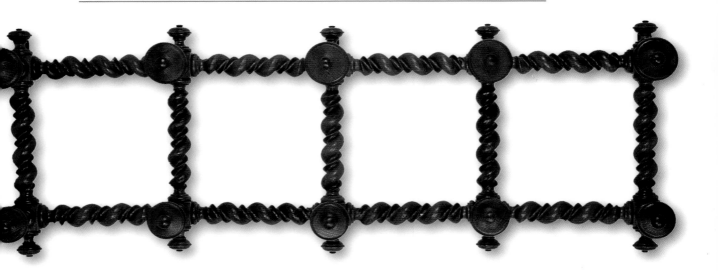

Very unusual hat rack for ten Derbies. A rectangular frame is constructed of twist-turned spindles with two rows of five projecting posts and larger round ends to hold the hats. $900-1000

Round umbrella stand made by the George Hunzinger Company of New York. At the top, a collar of two round and molded oak bands frame an intertwined oak frieze. The collar rests on vertical twist-turned spindles and a solid round base with four ball feet. A brass round dish fits on the round base. 11.5" d. x 27" h. No price available

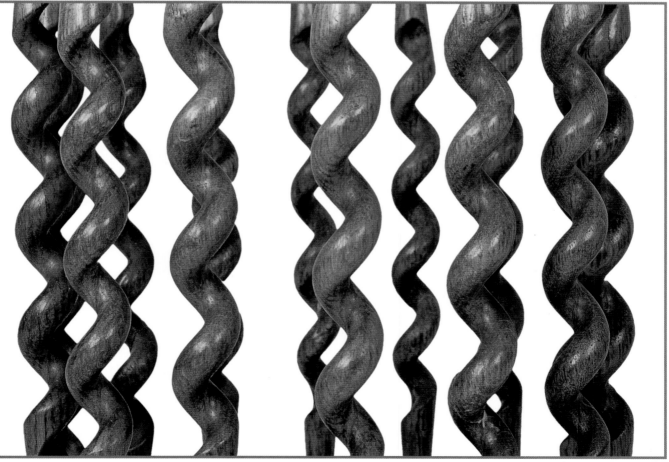

Umbrella stand with square frame and ball turned finials and feet. Round bent wood joins the frame and oak grillwork surrounds a metal base plate. 9" square x 27"h. No price available

Three-panel folding screen draped with tapestry
showing a fishing scene and green cloth panels.
Each panel in oak frame 18.5″ w. x 67.5″ h. $500-575

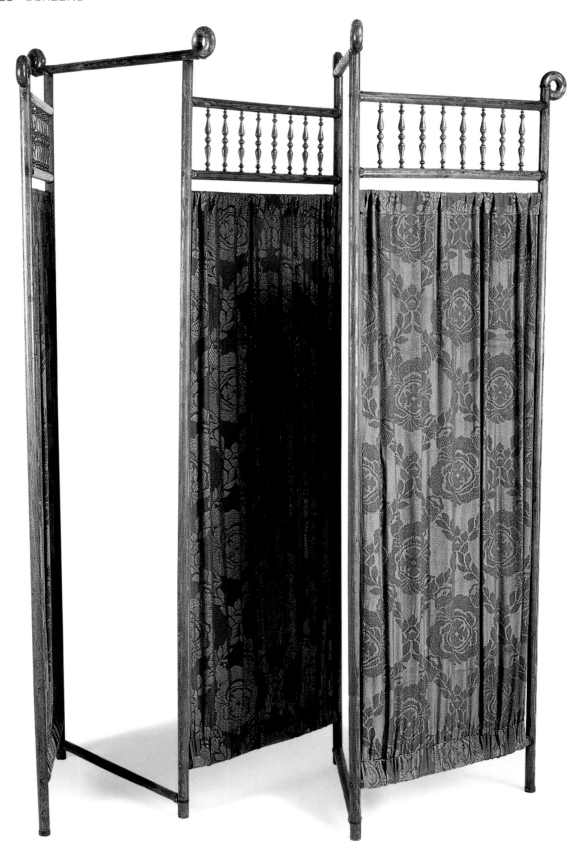

Five-panel dressing screen with spindle turnings and draped cloth. c. 1890. 63" h. $700-800

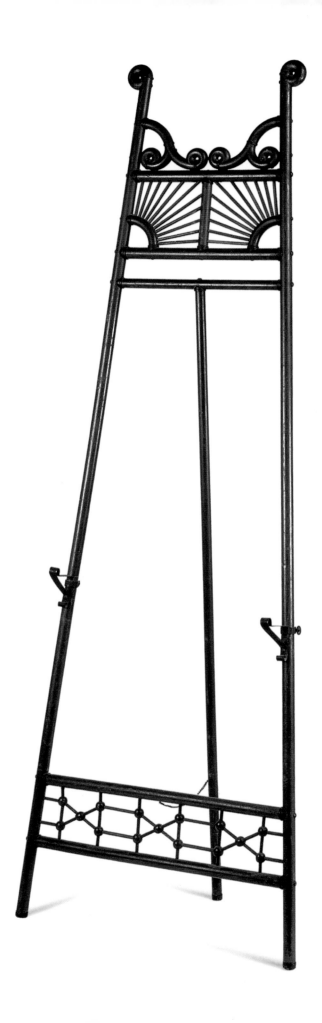

Easel with oak supports and decorative stick and ball turnings. c. 1880. 68" h. $700-800

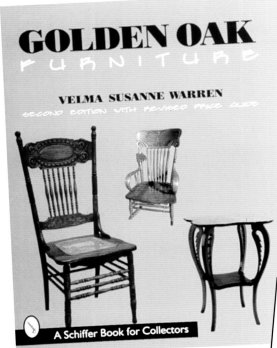

AMERICA'S OAK FURNITURE

SECOND EDITION WITH PRICE GUIDE

A Schiffer Book for Collectors

AMERICA'S OAK FURNITURE
REVISED 2ND EDITION
Nancy Schiffer
Over 300 photos of oak furniture illustrated in color and arranged by types, from armoires to tables. Hundreds of chairs are shown to display the great variety of styles. Famous makers such as Larkin, Stickley, and more are well represented. A current price guide makes it even more useful to collectors.
8 1/2" x 11"   300 color photos   Price Guide
128 pages   soft cover $24.95
0-7643-0580-8

American Wooden Chairs
1895-1908

The 1908 Catalog of the
Phoenix Chair Company
Sheybogan, Wisconsin

❖ Oak
❖ Walnut
❖ Elm
❖ More

A Schiffer Book for Collectors

With a Guide

[AME]RICAN WOODEN CHAIRS
[1895]-1910
[A fa]csimile of the detailed catalogue of the [Phoe]nix Chair Company with hundreds of de-[taile]d illustrations of American wooden chairs. [Rang]ing from golden oak to the Viennese-[style] bentwood, they show the variations and [diver]sity of American chair manufacturing. A [new] preface and a current price guide make [this] a valuable book for collectors and furni-[ture] historians.
[11" x] 8 1/2"   300 b/w illus   Price Guide
[128] pages   soft cover $29.95
[0-76]43-0374-0

FURNITURE MADE IN AMERICA
1875–1905
REVISED 4TH EDITION
Richard and Eileen Dubrow
An exhaustive compilation of all original catalog material from major American furniture manufacturers of the 1880s and 1890s. This is an important resource for identifying makers and understanding the range of their work. Included is furniture for the dining room, parlors, library, bedroom and office. Over 2000 illustrations and a price guide are included.
8 1/2" x 11"   2000 illus.   Price Guide
320 pages   soft cover $24.95
0-7643-0595-6

E&R DUBROW
FURNITURE
MADE IN AMERICA

A Schiffer Book for Collectors

1875~1905
4th Edition with revised Price Guide

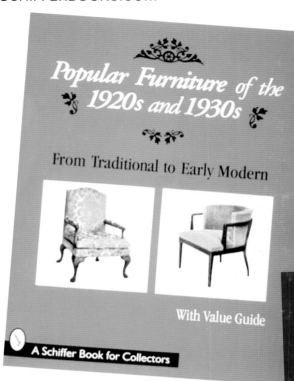

POPULAR FURNITURE OF THE 1920S AND 1930S

A facsimile edition of the Elgin A. Simonds Company's furniture catalog provides an extensive resource of the furniture styles of the 1920s and 1930s. Ranging from traditional to Art Deco, captions include important information about size, materials, and the period of the reproduction. Current values of the furniture have been added to make this book a useful addition to the collector's library.
8 1/2" x 11"   863 b/w photos   Price Guide
226 pages   soft cover $29.95
0-7643-0431-3

AMERICAN MANUFACTURED FURNITURE
REVISED 3RD EDITION
Don Fredgant

A mammoth representation of products of American furniture manufacturers. Hundreds of illustrations show the styles of furniture available at height of the 1920s, a pivotal period between Art Nouveau, Art Deco, and the Depression eras. A price guide and four indices make it an easy to use guide for collectors.
8 1/2" x 11"   Hundreds of illustrations
Price Guide/4 Indices   464 pages
soft cover $37.50
0-7643-0059-8

PINE FURNITURE
THE COUNTRY LOOK
Nancy N. Schiffer

The pine furniture and tools gathered in this have come from distant places in Europe United Kingdom, and Scandinavia. Painted cheerful colors, they served every practical tion. Over 280 beautiful color photographs construction details and furniture design of variety, so popular in homes today.
8 1/2" x 11"   284 color photos   price guide
144 pages   soft cover $29.95
0-7643-0742-8